Look at
Norway!

ARNE BESKOW

Look at Norway!

WITH AN INTRODUCTION BY
PIO LARSEN
AND LINE DRAWINGS BY
HANS GERHARD SØRENSEN

GYLDENDAL NORSK
FORLAG

© Gyldendal Norsk Forlag A/S 1981
Printed in Norway
Aske Trykkeri AS, Stavanger 1986
The pictures are printed
on 170 gr. Phönix Imperial
Design: Gunnar Lilleng
ISBN 82-05-13081-7

This is a love-story, — in pictures. It is dedicated to all the many hundreds of Norwegians, from Lindesnes to Kirkenes/Grense Jakobselv, who gladly took their time off in order to tell me about, and to show me, their favorite spots:

Places where to re-charge their own batteries, where answers to the many difficult questions of today are being found, and where word-less one-man-sermons humbly are being performed.

During four years I have been driving some 70,000 kms. or 45,000 miles, along and across Norway, mostly from April to October. Still, I have not been able to achieve anything more than a very few, superficial, glimpses from this, to me, most beautiful country.

This privilege of being allowed to make pictures from «all» of Norway, turned into one of the richest, and also one of the hardest, experiences in my life. And during the editing, of thousands of pictures, it did seem fairly easy to get them down to a number of about 800.

But from there on, to reach the final 200 pictures, progressive torture became the order of the day.

I tried to look upon it as a gardener, for whom a job well done also means trimming and weeding, but for every picture that disappeared, I felt as if I were assaulting something alive. Who am I to decide what is representative or not, and in a country of such unbelievable beauty? The publisher tried to comfort me, by saying that it had to be done, after all, and who could possibly do it less badly than the one who so intensely had lived through it all.

I plead guilty! All I can say for myself is that I have really tried to do my very best, even if the result is limited to how Norway appeared through my own eyes.

Some of the pictures were easy to take: Luck, in combination with first-class equipment and, of course, necessary technical knowledge.

Other pictures seemed impossible from the beginning: Dragging the heavy equipment up steep mountain-sides is routine, and so is the waiting, sometimes for hours, in snow, rain, fog, or hard winds. And to descend with no result at all, frozen and wet, is sometimes also part of the game. All there is to it is to try again the next day, or the day after, too, if necessary.

But sometimes I wondered if the trolls had put a spell upon me: Either I could not get the picture to sing, or suddenly that longed for and so very special light, just was not there anymore.

Not easy then to remember all the times, when both the picture and the light were served for free, on a platter.

As you know the Norwegian national anthem begins with the words: «Yes, we do love this country» . . .

So do I! But before you dismiss that statement as chauvinism, may I respectfully point out that I am a Swede, in love with my own country, too. That is why the statement is entirely personal, and no dreamed up promotional gimmick.

My name is printed as if I, alone, were responsible for this book.

I have but made the pictures!

That they made Pio Larsen enthusiastic, also to write about them, is marvellous. As is the presence of Hans Gerhard Sørensen's lovely drawings. All of it was done in very close cooperation and friendship, for which my humble «thank you very much» most certainly is not enough.

I do wish that the book by itself could tell about what a rare privilege it has been, to be part of it. Because of the publisher who all the time, and with no limits, offered support and encouragement in the most touching ways. THANK YOU VERY MUCH!

STOCKHOLM, IN APRIL 1981

Arne Beskow

Thule, Nåri, Nuruiak, Norvegr, Noregi, Norge, the Land of the North . . . How many were the names! From 325 BC, when Pytheas of Massilia reached Trondheim, after a journey no doubt deserving the then unknown expression of «a Viking tour». Right up to present days, when the battle is raging whether to print «Norge» or «Noreg» on the stamps. Even today the linguists are far from an agreement upon the actual meaning of the name. «No, not the land to the North», say some of them, «but the Road to the North».

Which all was completely indifferent to those animals and humans that went North, once the final ice age at last had come to an end. For them their course was simply set by the vegetation, which earlier and gradually had moved northwards; by the existence of life in the fjords and along the rugged coastline, formed by ice ages over a million of years; and by the animal and plant life, at last having found shelter after some 2,400 meters of courageous climbing upwards.

Once there, they all discovered that this Northern country was not at all so barren and deserted, as those in the lowland to the south believed. Following the road to the North, one could come across flaming poppies, sturdy little plants having survived the ice age, and now defiantly poking their heads through crevices in the highest peaks. And the animals of the tundra were in their natural environment long before humans, having moved northwards as do the lemmings on their last journey towards the sea. Wild reindeer, mountain foxes and snow owls, mountain grouse, snow sparrows, not to mention the lemmings; in the northern coastal areas and inner Trøndelag there was so much bare ground even in the ice age, that the lem-

mings managed to survive. A few Polar bears wandered over the glaciers, and as far south as Gudbrandsdalen the remains of mammoths, — those furry elephantine animals, which for some unknown reason are extinct, — even today inspire awe and respect. Just a few years ago, an arrow was found in this same area of Gudbrandsdalen, pierced in a glacier as if it had gone astray when shot from a bow thousands of years ago.

Flora and fauna are not constant, nor are even fjords and mountains. Just as the mammoth disappeared, so did mountain peaks as they tumbled into the sea, winding rivers became deep and narrow fjords, and quiet pools became big lakes. The moving, enormous ice masses were mainly responsible for these creations, but fiery volcanoes and earthquakes also made their contributions. While man and beast worked their way further and further north, as far as the fairy lands of the midnight sun, with their nights free from fear.

During this period Galdhøpiggen raised itself to its full height, followed by many others, like Glittertind, Memurutind, and Surtningssui. And certain lakes became close to inland-seas, like Mjøsa, or curiosities were formed such as Hornindalsvatnet. Which is the deepest lake in Europe, a recent survey showed that it was half a kilometer to the bottom. And as the ice gradually moved on, being a slave to the force of gravity, wide, deep rivers such as the Glomma were formed.

Very slowly Norvegr, the road to the North, became more: a country, a people, a nation. And it became a friendly country, because the warming and life-giving Gulf Stream took the same course.

The explosive volcanic eruptions and earthquakes ceased; with that terrifying period now existing only in the twilight of past history. And man and beast could settle down.

So could the plants. After a while there were about 1,300 different wild plants in Norway, not including the more remote species. But it wasn't always like that, far from it. The first species probably came from Denmark and Skåne. The basic trees were mostly birch, hazel and pine; plants included moss and dryad flowers.

It was similar with the animals. First came a few, almost an advance troop. Then gradually, as the temperature rose and the woods grew bigger, others appeared: wolverines, elk and bears, hares and lynx, field mice, voles, stoats, and thrushes. Finally, as a nature's jest, deer, badgers, hedgehogs, polecats, black grouse, common buzzard, all animals usually belonging to more southern areas.

The Land to the North, Norway, had become a beautiful country. Mountains rose steeply from glittering fjords, and rivers and waterfalls cascaded from the heavens or wound their ways through green valleys.

But Beautiful? There is little reason to believe that people in those days ever used such a word, if it really existed in the vocabulary of the Stone Age. The main appeal of the Land of the North was the opportunities for existence, the challenge of a continual battle between man and nature. There was hardly any beauty in whirling snowstorms and freezing nights, in wide, dangerous rivers which trapped hunters on the opposite bank, in animals which just disappeared, and in meagre berries and herbs that gave one pangs of hunger. One could seldom tell whether a hunter who left at dawn, would return at night. And in battle with the bears, all too often the king of woods became the winner.

But what about the people along the coast, did they fare any better? What about the fish, the seabirds, the eggs, the mussels? Certainly the archaeologists have discovered whole banks of mussel shells and remains of fish bones, which indicate a somewhat richer life. But beauty? Death by starvation or exposure was common. And when the winter hurricanes ravaged, and the sea pounded over the beaches right through the living quarters, death was playing the organ, indifferent to the reasons for lives thus becoming extinguished. Yet, some few people still survived, but one day there were no more mussels, forcing them, too, to move on to new territory.

Nothing strange at all, then, that these people developed a religion governed by the gods of nature — and that the sun-wheel became its symbol. When winter ended and the sun again appeared over the mountain-crests, no one was in doubt — here was their god, the one who with omnipotence ruled over man and beast.

Gradually Stone Age man became a recognizable human being, who could settle down and cultivate his land. No longer was he forced to live from hand to mouth, from now on he could begin to think of future generations. Very slowly a rural society grew up.

The latent sense of beauty was probably aroused at about this time. While, until now, one had been content with rather primitive rock-carvings, people now started to decorate their homes, their clothes, and their tools. Bards sang their praises of both master and fair maidens — perhaps this was when it became common for man and maid to take a rest in the hills, sitting on the green grass amongst the wild flowers, admiring the view, and capturing the vision in their hearts.

Perhaps love between man and woman developed from it all? Was this the birth of romance, as we know it in our days? We do not know. We only know that such phenomena as romance and love are fairly modern, something which is proved to us by science.

What has this to do with nature? Nothing more than that man's feelings and behaviour often are reflected by the nature surrounding them. Just look at the little girl in the mountains, clutching a bunch of lilies of the valley with chubby fingers, and with her quiet and so tranquile smile. Or for that matter, the ageing master-hunter of the village. With a body that is bent but still as strong and tough as a dwarf-birch, and with his so blue eyes almost transparent from many years of searching among far-away mountain-crests. And compare him with our modern city-man, who now is well on his way to lose this contact and solidarity with nature.

The scents from a lovely cloudberry marsh are now considered as of no importance at all, compared to the need for one more express-way. To conserve a mountain full of birds, a miracle in itself and right in the centre of Ålesund, is considered as unimportant where construction for a local police station is at stake. Several waterfalls are now no more than a name, and even far out in the wilderness complete clean-cutting is advocated as being rational and profit-friendly. It seems that man has gone backwards, to the Stone Age attitude of nature being an enemy. Is it really impossible to reverse this development, to revise our attitudes and, above all, to restore our contacts with creation?

Certain trends now do seem to give grounds for optimism.

And so — welcome to this journey through Thule, Nuruiak, Norvegr, Norge the Land to the North.

Or perhaps we should think in old-fashioned terms and follow the road to the North.

Norway's southernmost point is naturally in Sørlandet (Sør = South), therefore it is all the more curious that this part of the country not always has had this name. Up until 1902 it was called Vestlandet, but that year the poet Vilhelm Krag wrote an article about this in the newspaper «Morgenbladet», and from that day onwards, there was «Sørlandet».

Both in lyrical works and in daily speech, Sørlandet is often called «the soft coast», and there is some truth in this, both phonetically and geographically. The language has soft consonants, which often remind one of Danish, and the scenery is not typical Norwegian either. Anyway, nowhere else in Norway can one find such idyllic coastal scenery, — a holiday paradise.

However, «the soft coast» does not give a complete description. Lives can be at stake when the storms come in from the sea. Countless are the ships that during the years have gone down in the skerries. And countless are the heroic deeds done by the local population, lead by the pilots, in sea rescue work.

But Sørlandet is not just a coast. The mountain areas of Øvre Sirdal, Åseral, and parts of Setesdal, also belong to Sørlandet, and the mountain area from Rogaland over the moors of Sirdal and Setesdal are more and more often referred to as the moors of Sørlandet.

IX

While the poets of Sørlandet were writing sentimentally about their «soft coast», a very different key was used by our literary giant, Knut Hamsun, when he wrote about Oslo. In 1890 his novel «Hunger» was published, his sombre tale about «this strange city, which nobody leaves until he is marked by it».

It may well be that geographically Oslo is one of the larger cities in the world, but today hardly anyone is looking at Oslo with the eyes of Knut Hamsun. On the contrary, Oslo is no doubt one of the most peaceful and idyllic capital cities in the world.

Today about 500,000 people live in Oslo. Compared to the 12-16,000,000 living in New York, Tokyo, etc., both Oslo and the whole of Norway show up in their extravagance, in a world of population explosion and migration. Norwegians can go jogging or skiing even in the town centres, and they can go for a walk straight from their front doors, staying away for eight days without meeting a soul, if that's what they really want. This kind of freedom is a tourist attraction in itself. In addition to which Norway has very few pollution problems.

Not that we have succeeded completely to avoid this plague of civilization, but compared to any other industrialized country, we have not much to complain about.

The clouds in the sky have their natural colour, and right outside the city boundaries — and often inside as well — one can breathe in clean, fresh air. And if you avoid the most exposed water courses, you can still kneel on the banks, lean on the clean boulders, and quench your thirst with sparkling, pure water. An aristocratic luxury, just ask the tourists, they gladly pay a high price for the experience.

The clouds . . . does something like a true Norwegian sky really exist? Many people say so, especially artists and photographers., When the weather forecast includes «changing skies, it is not at all just empty talk. Who should know more about such things than artists, who claim that very few places in the world offer such dramatic changes in the sky as Norway. If a high pressure is building up west of Ireland, it is right here, above our Norwegian heads, that the skies tremble and moan. And if a low pressure is building up over the Kola peninsula, it is the Norwegians who feel the effect. Black, white, and dark grey clouds fight over Norwegian territory, the one formation chasing the next one across the skies. Rain is pouring down the one minute, the sun burning the next, unless, of course, it starts to snow, even in the middle of the summer. No wonder Norwegian painters are experts on clouds.

Everybody knows that Oslo is Norway's capital, but the city is also the centre on a more local plane, like, say, Trondheim in Trøndelag. Not only are the surrounding districts included, but also the whole of Østlandet (Øst = East), though it is impossible to define the exact boundaries. Which, vaguely, could be said to be Gudbrandsdalen in the north, the Swedish border in the east, Telemark in the west, and, of course, the sea in the south. It doesn't really matter. What is certain, however, is that Østlandet, or more accurately the county of Østfold, was the very first part of the country to become populated after the ice age. Nowhere else in Norway are found so many rock carvings, and the biggest burial mounds are to be found here, too. The remains of some forty iron age fortresses have also been discovered, indicating invasion and migration.

But Østfold can also show us how land was formed. It has no mountain areas, no terrifying gorges, and no dark and narrow fjords. The landscape consists mainly of flat country with a few hills, the highest one reaching only 327 meters. It has a favourable climate, oats grow in 96 days, quicker than anywhere else in Norway, and the fields start turning green in the middle of April. Blue anemones have been found on sunny hillsides as early as March 22.

What is the reason for these favourable conditions, with regard to the soil and the topography? The scientists state that parts of Østfold probably were below sea level at the end of the ice age. Which should have happened at the same time as the glaciers came tumbling southwards, melting in the warm climate. And thus land was formed, created by the deposits of clay and sand. The glaciers also formed moraines, some of them enormous, for example the one that runs from Jeløy in the northwest to Kornsjø in the southeast. But there is not much of typical Norwegian scenery; high mountains, deep valleys, and narrow fjords, to be found in Østlandet. On the other hand, the scenery is softer, rich in woodlands, with wooded ridges forming jagged horizons, one after the other, fading into the distance. Large expanses of the district mainly consist of forests, but far north in Hedmark rounded mountains become the dominating feature of the landscape. If you visit this woodland area, you will no doubt agree with the man who had studied the encyclopaedia: «It says here that 27% of Norway's area is covered by woods. But why doesn't it say that all of it is found in one place, right here?»

Which is how large areas of Østlandet do appear. But further north, the forest is more open, the higher up one comes. The mountains are still friendly, not yet cutting into the sky with sharpened peaks. Instead they peacefully heave above the moss, the tablelands, and over wide valleys and lakes.

Stone Age man probably chose a route going northwest, but hardly was he looking for beautiful scenery. He had to provide food for his family, why he followed the tracks of large and small animals; reindeer, elk, lynx, wolfes and bears, probably also mammoths. And as the animals found a natural way northwards, man followed after on safe and suitable tracks. Probably they went along the lake Mjøsa and through Gudbrandsdalen, where the simultaneous arrival of man and beast might have caused confusion. Because, to the west loomed «the proudest mountains of Northern Europe», as an author wrote later, and northwards there were mountains, too, blocking the way. Which route should they choose?

It was really much worse for the animals, though, with man close behind, flashing stone clubs or bows and arrows. So to begin with they chose «the proudest mountains»-way, Jotunheimen, as the poet Aasmund Olavson Vinje would call it many years later. Anyway, Jotunheimen remained unknown until well into the 19th century. That is «unknown to others than hunters, fishermen, or shepherds», again quoting Vinje. It wasn't until 1820, when Professor Baltazar Mathias Keilhau made a journey through Jotunheimen and described the area for the first time, that people began to show interest for it. But then it quickly became almost fashionable, for those with enough of leisure time, to wander from mountain to mountain all summer long. But many years had to pass before a map was produced over the area, and the man responsible for that achievement was N.S. Wergeland, later promoted to the rank of general. The map had to be read with a certain sceptisism, though, since Wergeland's instruments were rather primitive, why for example 90 meters were added to the height of Galdhøpiggen. Anyway, the map marked a new era. The foot tourist came into being. After 1860 it became almost common for foreigners and town people to spend their holidays in Jotunheimen. Which has been the name for this area, between Gudbrandsdalen and Sogn, since 1861. The name, Jotunheimen, wasn't a new one in the Norwegian language. It was first used in the Norwegian-Icelandic mythology, and later, strangely enough, for the flat areas surrounding the White Sea, in Russia.

Generations would succeed generations before this stage was reached. The very first men to walk among these colossal mounds of stone, probably felt as disoriented as the very first men on the moon. As hunters they had their keen, natural instincts, and knew how to survive, but they had a fear of the dark, an irrational fear that sent shivers down the back of even the bravest of men. Imagine the feelings of Stone Age man and his family, when dark fell and they had to make their way along steep trails with precipitous drops on either side. And there were other dangers, too, — hungry wolves and bears, the gods, of course, and the spirits of the dead!

As if the mountains weren't threatening enough by day, all you needed was to tread wrongly just once! Wandering across Jostedalsbreen, the largest glacier in Europe, one could (and still can) easily find one's grave at the bottom of a deep crevice, where one would die of cold or hunger, if one wasn't killed instantly. Or what about storms, and thunder and lightning, which could cause an avalanche? Or slice down huge pieces of disintegrating rock, falling down in great boulders, threatening their settlements? And as all of this was quite possible during daytime, what couldn't then happen at night?

No, the first people to enter these mountainous areas most certainly were no tourists. And never would they have understood anyone who considered the mountains as magnificent and beautiful.

But then, on a precipice looking west, Stone Age man stops, sniffing the air like an animal. What is this? A new smell, fresh and salty! At least a new smell he thinks, and on this day perhaps he can afford to be a little curious, too. So, waving to his family, he grunts that he will be making a detour, to find out from where the smell is coming.

And from now on, anything can happen.

Perhaps man first chose a southern route, leading him on to Jostedalsbreen, perhaps fate led him further west, why he arrived in Vestlandet. And if he was lucky enough to find the route via Geiranger, he had found the route made by nature and many were to follow in his tracks.

Although impressive roads have been built today, such as Ørneveien (the Eagle road), or the 16 km long road to Geiranger (the latter bringing artistry to road-building, with all its hairpin bends), much remains of the wild countryside that Stone Age man met. There are waterfalls, well known to tourists all over the world, such as the Bridal Veil, and the Seven Sisters. Which still are allowed a free fall straight down into Geirangerfjorden. And the mountain-sides are still as steep, and the fjords as narrow, that no ship was allowed to use its siren, for fear of causing an avalanche.

And if you bend your head far back, looking way up to the ledges, high above the steep mountain-sides, you can see remains of old farms, only accessible to climbers one would think. Poverty made people settle here, often with good results, and some of the farms were still being cultivated after the last war.

But Stone Age man could not see any beauty in all this. For example, Flydalsjuvet — the beautiful gorge which is famous today — was regarded only as a threat in those days. An excellent place for executions, though: if you pushed a man over the edge, his remains would probably never be found in the rubble several hundred meters below. But for anything else the gorge was useless. No. Stone Age man now continues his hunt for that strange, salty smell, which is getting stronger every day. A good thing it is coming from the west, because south and eastwards there are only mountains to be seen, their peaks as close to each other as arrows in a quiver. Today this area is known as Sunnmørs-alpene, but their snow-capped peaks had no appeal to Stone Age man: a good place for birds, perhaps, but a bird is not an easy target, however tight the arrow is strung on the bow.

But if Stone Age man thinks that he will find somewhere without mountains, he is going to be disappointed.

He has literally come to a land of mountains. They cover nearly ¾ of Norway, and even today only 2% of the land is cultivated. One should here perhaps also take into account the 150,000 islands, spread along the coast like peppercorns. But they hardly make any difference, only 2,000 of them are inhabited, and most of those people earn their living from the sea, not from the land.

But mountains can be so many things, from the gentle hills in Østfold, to the titanic, black tusks and fangs in the county of Møre og Romsdal, as well as further up in the northern counties.

All these mountains have reached much deeper into the Norwegian souls than even the poets have realized. The shapes of the mountains have always appealed to the imagination, giving grounds for religious beliefs, not to mention the superstition all these masses of stone have been responsible for, right up until today. It was no whim causing man to name a range of mountains to Trolltindene, «The Troll Peaks», there was serious reasoning behind it. And imagine Styggedalstind, «Peak of the Bad Valley», Torshammeren, «Thor's hammer», Troll-steinseggi, «Edge of the Trolls' Rock», and Kyrkja, «The Church», to name but a few. The experts have much to tell about the subject. Another country-wide phenomenon is how people imagine that they do see faces, carved out of the rock. Bjørn-stjerne Bjørnson seems to appear again and again, followed by swarms of minor dignitaries. Or one may see the shapes of animals or objects, such as the Pulpit, at Geiranger and Lysefjorden. Nobody has ever preached from those rocks, but as seen from below, they really do look like a pulpit.

Although Norway doesn't have the very highest mountains in the world, here is where you find some of the most treacherous, obviously attracting both foreign and Norwegian climbers. And every year some fatal accident happens. But the mountains can be fatal in other ways, too: snow drifts and avalanches are common. There is no country in the world where rescue preparations are made to such a degree, during holiday periods, as in Norway. Unfortunately Norway is also a country where mountain peaks suddenly disintegrate and fall into the sea, as in Tafjord in 1934. As a consequense gigantic tidal waves crashed through the villages, and 41 lives were lost. There were two similar accidents in Loen, in 1905 and 1936. With the floods then claiming 134 lives, completely destroying the villages of Nesdal and Bødal. As the area still is regarded as dangerous, no ships are allowed to enter.

But surely the mountains will and do show themselves from a completely different aspect, much more generous and friendly. Sometimes the snowy mountains will appear with a sparkling intensity, as if on a painting by Weidemann. Although there appears to be no vegetation, the stone seems to come to a glittering life with a lot of colours — purple, darkgreen moss, and rust-red moors. Lower down there are dwarf birches, rare mountain flowers, and perhaps a little pool, nestled among the birch- and willow-thickets. And as the sun beats down, one is tempted to strip to the waist, even the cool breeze has been warmed by the sun as it caresses one's bare skin.

Fast-moving between these utter extremes of temper, the mountains accepted or rejected the arrival of Stone Age man, the hunter, in exactly the same way as today they accept or reject modern man, the tourist. And our Stone Age man wandered further on, westwards, up the steep slopes, and down again, always in rugged country, always with a stony ground to walk on. Until one day . . .

There he is, on the edge of a cliff, surrounded by women and children, raising his arm and pointing like Moses: There! The promised land!

No doubt that even the very first immigrants realized the significance of all this. Out there, by the sea, they would be able to find an existence. There would be a lot of fish, and that there would be good hunting on the beaches they already knew. But it would take quite some time before they realized that this water was the endless ocean, and that the sea would demand much more from them than they were used to. And it would take a long time before they came to understand how very dependant they were upon the weather on the coast. But learn they did — as archaeological finds have proved. Close to Ålesund, several years ago, were discovered a number of flint implements, much of which was confirmed as being fishing-tackle.

Few countries do offer such natural phenomena as the fjords in Norway, and it is easy to see why these fjords have become one of the biggest tourist attractions. To create fjords, two conditions are vital: the landscape must be dominated by ranges of mountains, and the land had to be massively covered by ice during the last ice age. In Norway those conditions were fulfilled, as they were in Greenland, Alaska, British Columbia, Patagonia, New Zealand and in Scotland.

But it seems that those countries are more or less ignored when tourists talk about fjords. One reason why the tourists from Japan or France, for example, immediately think of Norway is perhaps that we by far have the most and the longest fjords. And because of the Gulf Stream, some of the country around the fjords is also incredibly fertile. Which together with that the surrounding scenery is some of the very wildest and most beautiful, results in a very strange combination, indeed. Fjords are to be found along the whole of the coastline, that is to say in several climatic zones. The soil covering the steep mountain slopes, rising from the fjords, frequently is of a quality by far surpassing that of most gardens. But that is not all. A fjord within a favourable climatic area, that is with a lot of sun, will be almost like a greenhouse. And the luxuriance of the vegetation is something the tourists find hard to believe.

While our forefathers may not have been appreciative of the beauty of their surroundings, they soon found out other qualities, offered by the fjords. The abundance of fish was one thing, of course, but of the same importance was the discovery that the fjords also could be used as means of communication. With an errand to do inland, no more need to embark upon a hazardous journey up and down the mountain slopes. No reason to get stuck up there any more, searching for the easiest road. Much better to get into their little boats, made of hides, for a pull along the silk-smooth searoad. And what did it matter if a storm blew up, the nearest beach was always close by.

But communication was not at all limited only to the fjords. The long coastline became the main road of Norway, and before long people also left the coast for the open sea. Archaeological finds, especially in Sogn og Fjordane, have proved that there was communication between Norway and Shetland, Scotland, Isle of Man, and Ireland. In fact, Sogn og Fjordane is the county with the most of archaeological finds from other countries. From which so many quiet tales are told, about dreams, courage, and boldness when facing the cruel sea.

This was of course later, but even Stone Age man was not alone on the coast. Man's neighbour was perhaps a long way off, but in return he was surrounded by animal life in abundance. Seals, for example, meant much more than food for the family. The menu was expanded with such items as puffins, eagle-owls, razor-bills, common guillemot, kittiwakes, eider ducks and seagulls. But the joyful wheatear, jester of the skies, only 15 cm long, and quicker than an arrow, was usually left in peace to sing its rebellious song at night. And when food was scarce, people probably ate things which were easily obtained from the beach, such as seaweed and tansy.

Perhaps the coastal vegetation was much richer. It has been proved that not all of Norway was covered by snow and ice during the last ice age, by the discoveries of certain fossils, found both on the west and the north coast. And some of the plants, to be found there today, too, have probably survived the many changes of climate in their original forms. Another strange thought: Was Norway joined to the British Isles at one time? Some people believe so, stating that there must have been some sort of botanical bridge between the two countries. And today there exist several kinds of plants which are to be found only in Norway and, for example, in Scotland.

But it is a known fact that most of the vegetation to be found in Norway has come from Sweden and Denmark. The process is still being carried on, as far as the spruce-tree is concerned. Not yet has the spruce reached the westcoast growing by itself, in spite of a favourable climate. On the other hand, pine, hazel and birch trees were to be found there as soon as the ice had retreated.

And ever since, forests have been the characteristic feature of the Norwegian landscape. Pine, spruce, and birch are the dominating kinds, being also of great importance to the country's economy. But other species contribute to the luxuriance: maple, elm, oak, ash, and poplar. And in the seaside town of Larvik are even found the remains of beech woods.

But the birch is the national tree of Norway. They can become very tall and majestic, to which is added their ermin-like, snow-white bark, and their crowns of green and gray. And their habit of growing anywhere is almost magical. They take over fields which have not been cultivated for some time, or a seed will find its way into a crack in the rock, so narrow that there's hardly room for a razor blade. The force of its growing power is tremendous, more than enough to widen the crack, and within a few years a luxuriant birch tree will be there, looking as if the roots were bedded in the rock.

While three quarters of Norway are covered with mountains, most of the remaining quarter consists of forests, including our birch growing from the rock itself.

These rich and natural resources are of course reflected in the traditions of building. Where in most other countries houses are built of stone, Norway has always used timber for building material. But timber doesn't last forever, why there are no really old buildings left in Norway. With the exception of the famous stave churches, of course, whose upkeep is a matter very, very close to the heart of every Norwegian.

People don't seem to realize how exiting Norwegian botany and vegetation really are. Take the peat, as an example, which fishermen on the Dogger Bank bring up. That peat tells us that once there must have been dry land — in other words it is further proof that once there was a bridge over the North Sea, maybe in prehistoric times. And how can one explain the spreading of certain mountain plants, for example the poppies? How can small seeds jump right over different climatic zones, to far away mountains? Even more strange it becomes when we realize that some of these plants are found only in Norway, why they cannot be immigrants.

One thing remains absolutely certain: if it hadn't been for its vegetation (the Gulf Stream), Norway would have been the epitome of all cold and barren countries. But do we know how to make the very best of our natural resources? In times long since passed trees were planted where needed, where no woods existed. And corn and vegetables were grown even where it seemed impossible. But today we Norwegians, too, continually see fertile land being covered with asphalt, and we see trees being chopped down to such an alarming extent that the result must be a coming erosion. And yet, we are by far better off than most other countries in the world, by still having so much left of our natural resources.

Did the Stone Age people have any competition out there on the coast? Did more immigrants come from the east and south to settle in the same districts, leaving little room for the first settlers? One would have thought that there was room for them all, but those who are dependent upon fish and wild animals, berries and herbs, do need a lot of space. Whatever the reason, one group of people must have been the first to break away and move on.

Perhaps the reason was that they had noticed the sun? And that the days seemed longer in one place than in another? Was there not then reason to believe that the nights would become shorter, the further north they travelled? That, in fact, there might be a new world up there, with no nights at all?

Maybe no one really believed this, but what did they have to lose? Nothing much, really. And if they could find a land without nights, there would be no fear either, they would have left the evil spirits behind them.

So off they go again — northwards this time — and sure enough, the nights grow shorter, and the dreams of the land of light grow stronger. Many settle in Trøndelag. The landscape seems friendly, no more of the dramatic and scary wildness, there are animals to be hunted and fish in the sea. And besides, the days have become longer — in the summer. On the other hand, the nights have become longer, much longer, in the winter. And when the clouds quickly gather together above them, like hides being pulled over their heads, and day and night are as one, then it is really frightening. On such days even the old, wise ones are silent, and if a storm breaks loose, they all anxiously huddle together in their caves. One just cannot escape from the evil spirits.

But soon a new summer chases the dark thoughts away, and our wanderers move on. Further and further north they go, the dark nights almost disappear, and one day they stop and say — Here, this is the place, we have arrived! Why here exactly? From the hill they look down upon a new world, with thousands of islands scattered in the sea, almost like fish scales. Thousands of islands? They have no idea. Even today no one is quite sure about exactly how many islands there are in Nordlandsleia, Lofoten, and Vesterålen. Men of learning are still crouching over aerial photos, counting and counting, but never will they reach the correct total.

The next thing the immigrants notice is the amount of fish. When the cod comes in toward land, it can literally be scooped up with bare hands, and soon is also found the way to catch herrings. Seine fishing comes into existence. And the main features of the shore sein have remained unchanged from prehistoric times until today.

But has man been in too much of a hurry? After a while people begin to worry again. No doubt that there is more than enough of fish and seafare to be had, in fact one could exist from just collecting eggs if necessary. But as the islands are so close together, with only narrow passages between them, there are very strong currents, dangerous to even the biggest boats. No doubt that many a tragic accident was the reason why those currents gradually got their names: Gimsøystraumen, Sundklakkstraumen, Nappstraumen, Moskenesstraumen, to mention the most important.

And more shocks were in store. When winter hurricanes raged over the coast, it could be fatal just to go out of doors. An icy gust could throw one straight down into the sea — and to the waiting monsters.

Weren't we talking earlier about natural phenomena playing on our imagination? On the coast of North Norway, these phenomena more often are the rule than the exception. The islands, scattered along the coast so generously by the Creator, are not just friendly little rocks. When searching for a really wild landscape, nothing comes even close to that where steep mountains rise straight up from

the sea, looking like rows of the devil's teeth. Today science offers dry and nondebatable explanations as to how this rugged coast came into being. But in those days one saw what one saw, the rest was up to the imagination. Which is how the legends originated, about the mountain range Hestmannen (The Horseman), De Syv Søstre (The Seven Sisters), Torghatten (a mountain shaped like a hat with a hole in it), and Leka-møya (The Maiden of Leka). At that time there would have been no point in telling people that the hole in Torghatten had been dug out by stone and sea, at the end of the last ice age. Did you ever hear such nonsense? Everybody knew how it really did happen, but better to keep very quiet about it, one did not disturb the gods unpunished. There are several versions of this legend, and here is the most common one:

On Hestmannøy there is a mountain which from afar looks like a horseman, wearing a wide cape. These are the remains of a giant, who lived there in times gone by. At the same time some hundred kilometers further south, on the island of Leka, there lived a fair, female troll, to whom the giant proposed. But she was rather cocky, and refused him. She was also an expert in the use of magic, and all the people he sent to her, to plead his case, were skillfully turned into stones, still there. Finally the giant got so mad, that he took his bow and shot a gigantic arrow of stone. The arrow went right through Torghatten, thus losing its strength, and never reached the goal. But it is still there, today, a tall boulder resting right outside the north of Leka. The giant was very handy with magic, too, and the troll-girl of Leka and the giant on Hestmannøya used so many tricks fighting each other, that finally both of them turned into stone. And there they stand, angrily looking at each other, as they will until doomsday.

Another version of this story tells that one fine summer evening, the horseman saw the Leka maiden and her six sisters bathing naked. As he was used to getting whatever he wanted, he went after them. Shyness being what it was in those days, the seven sisters desperately fled southwards at the sight of him. But close to Alstahaug their strength was gone, and they collapsed, one after the other. The horseman then got so mad that he shot an arrow after the Leka maiden, the last of the sisters. This commotion woke up the noble king of Brønnøy, and when he saw the arrow coming, he threw his hat to stop it. The arrow went straight through, but soon fell to the ground. Whereupon the sun rose, and all the trolls of course immediately turned into stone.

Such legends abound, with more of them here in the north than anywhere else, and they may sound primitive. But the three counties of North Norway — Nordland, Troms, and Finnmark, have made more marks in Norwegian history than most other counties. During the times of the vikings, there were generations of families, continuously excercising great influence upon our art and culture. Øyvind Finnson Skaldspillar, one of Norway's greatest writers, came from here. As did Haarek from Tjøtta, one of the great viking chieftains.

The expression «full of contrasts» has nearly become a cliché where Norway as a whole is concerned, as frequently being used also for Sørlandet, Østlandet, and Vestlandet. But for North Norway the expression is really valid. The different seasons, for example: it is as frightfully dark in the winter, and for so long a heavy time, as it is happily light during the too short summer. The presence of the Gulf Stream upsets the use of temperature statistics:

what is felt as a windy but comparatively mild day at the sheltered coast, can be a screaming killer of a Polar storm, of unbelievable fury and coldness, whipping the sea into maelstroms of irregular frothy mountains, or, in the Finnmarksvidda, lashing the snow into a wailing twilight of the gods. Where, on a July-day, the temperature easily may rise so high that only the mosquitoes are stirring.

How the Lapps ever have managed to survive as a race in those dramatic circumstances, remains a mystery. But then it is claimed that the Lapps are the last of a race which also included the Indians of America. The theory being that originally these people came from Asia. Some of them managed to cross the Bering Straits, while others settled elsewhere, among them the Lapps, who came to Ultima Thule, furthest north. This theory is supported by the discovery in 1925, by the archaeologist Anders Nummedal, of the 10,000 year old settlement near Komsa in the Alta fjord. Be it Lapps — or the Stone Age men coming from the south, from wherever they came they certainly had their settlements, and why not in Komsa?

Finnmarksvidda! This tundra land, which on fine days can remind one of the endless prairies of the wild west, is a land where survival is a noble art. Today it looks exactly as it has been for thousands of years; slightly hilly plains, with rivers full of fish, and with endless swarms of mosquitoes. The vegetation consists mainly of dwarf shrubs and birch, which the Lapps cut down with their colossal knives, not unlike the machetes of Latin America. And who knows what still remains of the use of magic with the Lapps? It is scary to watch them making a sparkling fire from green, fresh twigs, using but one match.

There is grandeur about the north of Norway, a part of the world which has fostered some of the country's greatest writers, not to speak about the skilful fishermen and hunters. It is a world to which everyone who ever visited it, is longing to return. A world which ought to make us stop and think. Even if you go as far north as to Mo i Rana, for the midnight sun, you have only come half the way. Yet, all Norwegians, including the Lapps, are one and the same people. And, whatever other problems they may have, one basic thing they all have in common: the incredible scenic beauty, surrounding them all.

This makes it easier to understand that one of the great writers about North Norway, Carl Schøyen, came from Sørlandet. One summer as a boy he went to stay with his uncle, a lighthouse keeper on the island of Skomvaer, and he became fascinated with that part of the world. He was so impressed with the everlasting summer days that Jonas Lie's words could well have been his:

I headed east, I headed west
I headed I know not where
But no matter where I twisted and turned
It was northwards I always strayed.

Screaming killer of a Polar storm, whipping the sea into maelstroms . . . Exactly.

No one is better at complaining about the weather than a Norwegian. But send him to a country where the sun shines all the time, and he will soon get homesick.

— Give me water — begged Nordahl Grieg's seaman through parched lips, in the poem about the man sitting in a tropical bar, longing for home.

And most Norwegians living abroad, do feel the

same — their fondest memories of home always have something to do with water.

Their whole existence is connected with water, be it the sea itself or the drip from melting snow on a warm day at Easter. The wonderful drip of spring that will soon become a trickling brook, which in turn will run into other streams, finally becoming a powerfully rushing river. Almost every year some of these rivers flood their banks, drowning the fields, and sometimes whole villages are under water. But one forgets this. What one remembers is the purity the river symbolises, the refreshing feeling of being able to bathe one's face in cold, fresh water. Or the evening peace by the water: sitting by a bonfire on the shore, enjoying the twilight. Or being out in a boat, the silence broken only by the strokes of oars.

But, «Here the water is rushing away to no use». This was the text in the geography book, written below a picture of a beautiful, untamed waterfall. One can almost feel the author's despair over all this waste, how he looked at the cascading water and thought «just imagine how much electric power this waterfall could have yielded».

And his reasoning is of course correct, in a way. For economy's sake it is more important to have electricity than cascading waterfalls. But perhaps the day is not so far away when there are no waterfalls left to be directed through the power stations. When the national bird of Norway, the dipper, will have become an anachronism.

That the weather is very changeable in Norway, we've already talked about. A brilliant sunny day in May can suddenly change dark grey with pouring rain. Rain? No, it's hail! Or was, rather, because suddenly it's snowing heavily, with lightning and thunder as a strange accompaniment. Every organizer of sports is painfully familiar with these mad whims of the weather: A ski jumping competition is planned for a day in late winter, and participants have come from far and wide. And so have many Norwegian spectators, gathered to celebrate one more undoubtedly Norwegian victory. But no sooner has the opening fanfare been played than the rain starts to pour down, and the whole tower is hidden in a massive fog.

It doesn't matter too much when only sport events are affected, even if the organizers hardly share this opinion. But the brutal changes of the weather can also mean a danger to life. «He stayed out there» is the simple message, too often brought to the widows and children of seamen and fishermen. Unexpected storms and droughts also can cause tragedy to the farmers, in a few seconds, or during endless weeks of burning sun, destroying a fine harvest. Turning the expected family income into a bitter loss instead.

But in our memories, the endless summers of our Norwegian childhood were always warm and sunny. As were the Easter holidays at the log cabin, with the family. Norway was all sun in those days.

A statement which most certainly doesn't stand, so let us face the facts: surrounded by the sea, as most of Norway is, covered with mountains, and exposed to storms and winds from all directions, the unexpected does happen. One thing remains for a fact, though: never will the weather become boring.

This so very changing climate is reflected in many ways — just look at all the different plants: for example the purely tropical Monkey-scare tree that grows in Ålesund, of all places. As unbelievable a fact as the scientifically proved one about the bumble-bee being absolutely unable to fly. Orchids are found in the woods, and in a garden you will find all sorts of foreign plants. Including, as an example, the Rosa Wichuraina, a creeping rose with its home in East China.

Not so strange then, that Norway became populated some 10,000 years ago, maybe even earlier.

And that it was discovered that the land to the north was not so barren, after all.

And they all followed the road to the north, at least part of the way, continually discovering new features of this so very beautiful, and so very remarkable country.

New features, like the first wrinkles in a wise face . . .

Porten er åpnet —. Værsågod stig på!
Fra Briksdal, Sogn og Fjordane.
The door is open, - come on in!
From Briksdal, Sogn og Fjordane.

Også lyset kan her være glassklart
ofte blinkende som edelstener
Precious, sparkling stones sometime
seem to be added even to the air

En blankpolert vannflate, skog, fjell — i ett ord: Femunden.
With the surface polished and the mountains cleansed,
lake Femunden is ready for the party.

Ved bredden av Elgåa som har sitt utløp i Femunden,
kan man oppleve morgendisens sære karakter.
A true fairy-tale at Elgåa,
the small river on its way to Femunden.

Selv ikke treet er en isolert majestet.
Det glir inn i naturen, og blir som her formet av vinden.
This pine has turned into a wind-mobile.

«Morgenstund gir gull i munn» heter det. Her burde det lyde:
«Morgenstemning ved Femunden, har edelstener i bunnen.»
Are there diamonds at the bottom, too?

Og slik får hvert tre sin egen form, i en gnistrende
innramming av vann og av fjellets egne farger.
*Thus every tree gets its own shape, framed by all
the reflected colours from the water and the fjell.*

5

Morgenens første glans siger inn over Elgåa. ▷
The first bars of the morning-ouverture, being played at Elgå.

Kvelden senker seg over Fjellgutusjøen ved Femunden.
Evening-curtain going down. Lake Fjellgutusjøen by Femunden.

Morgenluften var som silke, mettet med fuktighet, og alt var musikk,
men så tyst at utløseren på mitt kamera lød som pistolskudd.
The morning air was like moist silk, and everything was music.
But so quiet that my camera sounded like a gun, going off.

Så kom regnet da over Glomma, like ved Jutulhogget,
og som jeg ruslet der i den bløte skogbunnen,
lå plutselig et Vår Herres blomsterarrangement foran meg.
Rain on the river Glomma, just behind Jutulhogget.
And as I walked through the wet woods,
suddenly a flower arrangement was in front of me.

En bjørk speiler seg i vannet nedenfor fossen, og også
vannet blir grønt. Fra Kleivafossen — Gravåsen ved Femunden.
Looking into the green mirror, what does
the little birch-tree really see? From Kleivafossen —
Gravåsen, close to Femunden.

Motiver fra Tron ved Alvdal, og en linje fra notisboken:
«Tron er som et stort rugbrød, som et kjempetroll
som ruslet langs Glomma, har lagt fra seg.»
The mountain Tron, (close to Alvdal), looks like
a huge piece of rye-bread, left by some gigantic troll.

Sollia kirke, slik som Vår Herre valgte å presentere den
for fotografen — og Rondane, slik dette fjellterrenget
fremstiller seg for fotturisten når været er i godt lune.
No wonder that the district of Rondane is close to the heart of all Norwegians.
Here with the Sollia-church resembling a rare amethyst.

Nattkvarter ved Atne-osen. Den klare kvelden lover frost,
men verten hadde lagt opp et stort lager av bjørkeved.
Night-stop for the tired but happy wanderer.
Atne-osen, near Koppang. Frost was in the air,
but my host had stocked an ample supply of firewood.

Rondane — her sett fra en side som turistene
sjelden opplever, de hektiske månedene da høsten
biter seg fast og gjør landskapet klart for vinteren.
A Rondane seldom seen by the summer-tourists:
The hectic days when Autumn is biting,
preparing the land for Winter's arrival.

Morgenstemning ved Fåberg i Gudbrandsdalen.
Morning at Fåberg. A train and a cow were singing a duet
as I came out from my overnight-cabin.

Som dyrebare fugleegg lå reinlaven en tidlig morgen trofast vernet om
av blåbærlyng som også kjente frosten bite i seg.
As if eggs from some rare bird,
the reindeer moss was faithfully guarded by the frosty blueberries.

Få steder i landet blir tradisjonene tatt vare på
som i Gudbrandsdalen, noe som denne stavkirken
i Ringebu er et levende eksempel på.
From Ringebu, in the valley of Gudbrandsdalen.
The lovely wooden church, from Viking times,
has much to tell, and is an example of well kept tradition.

19

Ved Engeren i Trysil. Skodden hadde nettopp begynt å slå sprekker,
så jeg ble værende der og satte opp stativet.
Om Mesterregissøren nå bare ville leke med spotlights fra solen.
Og det ville han.
At lake Engeren. The heavy overcast began to lift
and I set up the tripod in case the Master wanted to play with spotlights.
Which he did.

På vei nedover til Trysilelva. Jeg følte en dyp takknemlighet
over å ha fått oppleve alt dette. Og en verkende uro fordi
det ikke sto i menneskelig makt å yte det rettferdighet.
Near the river Trysilelva. My happiness, at being here right now,
was mixed with worries: Please, if possible, let me get all this
on my film, exactly as in this glorious moment.

Vann som leker seg med stein, siden alders tid en opplevelse ▷
for såvel store som små. Her blir kvister i fantasien til farkoster,
som en følger spent med øynene på den ville ferd.
Still by Trysilelva. A landscape? Or a dreamscape
launching one's fantasy into orbit?

Alle sanser våkner til liv i et område som dette.
Trysilelva er ikke bare vann, men den er skog langs breddene og tusen dufter
fra levende og råtnende planter, og suset fra elva og fra tusener insekter
gir også ørene et inntrykk som festner seg i minnet.
Trysilelva is so much more than just a river.
Huge forests, with the sounds and the smells of the living and the dying.
Insects, dancing around you by the thousand.
And birds, already having warned the elks of your presence.

Oppe på det hvitkalkede fjellet — Risørs sjømerke —
kunne jeg høre århundrenes røst: Jeg vil ut! Jeg vil ut!
O, måtte han bare komme hjem! Og de hvite husene berettet stille
om generasjoners forhåpninger, planer, glede og sorg.
On top of the white-washed mountain behind Risør,
I could hear the voices from long ago: «Soon, I will sail away, far away!»
«Please, let him come home safely!» And the white buildings quietly told about
the hopes, the plans, the joys, and the sorrows, of many generations.

26

Farsund —. Søndagsstillheten på havnen var fullkommen.
Farsund, where Sunday-peace reigned.

Listalandet, mykt, åpent og med en skjelvende klar luft,
gjorde det umulig å passere dette motivet.
Man ble kortpustet av den skjønnhet som omgav en. Og alt ble understreket,
poengtert av de fyrstelige fjellene i bakgrunnen.
The soft and open beauty of Lista-land emphasized
by the threatening mountains on the horizon.

Som i et ovalt brilleglass innrammes naturen
av bro og speilbilde.
Nature framed by bridge and reflections as if
viewed through binoculars.

Åkrafjorden og en ny venn. En kort samtale, en klype tobakk
og litt energisk kløing mellom hornene — og man har skaffet seg en kompis for livet.
*Åkrafjorden and a new friend. Small talk, a pinch of tobacco,
some friendly scratching, and the goat even tried to follow me into the car.*

Jøssingfjorden — karrig, hardt og bratt
— ikke tilrådelig for noen bilfører å slappe av et ørlite øyeblikk.
Om man aldri så mye befinner seg på historisk grunn.
*The Jøssingfjorden — barren, steep, austere — no place
for drivers to relax, though being on historical grounds.*

Elva har det travelt på sin ferd ned til Åkrafjorden.
This little river is certainly in a hurry to reach Åkrafjorden.

Et standardbilde for alle som bor på Voss. Men for oss andre,
som kjører denne veien som beveger seg i fine slyng,
blir begeistringen like stor hver gang vi
plutselig konfronteres med dette edle smykket.
An everyday sight for the good people of Voss. But for us,
just passing by in our cars, this precious jewel is handed over
as a most welcome reward. No grand-prix-driving
down the steep curves leading to this waterfall, no Sir!

Melselva ved Rosendal har vokst seg diger
etter fem døgns uavbrutt regn.
Men stedet kan friste den mest morgengretne
til å prøve fiskelykken.
The name of the river is Melselva.
You find it at Rosendal, right behind the Folgefonn.
A 4 kg salmon soon made the day for this fisherman.

Slik bor en ekte nordmann!
Homestead for a true Norwegian!

Aurland en tidlig morgen med striregn.
Og fra det høye skylaget fortsatte det å strømme ned,
mens ferja fra Gudvangen nærmet seg Aurland.
Aurland, an early morning in soft rain.
Still pouring down as the ferry from Gudvangen approached.   35

Fra Flåmsdalen, en gang i tiden utgangspunkt for en nesten uløselig oppgave
for landets jernbaneingeniører, i dag — ved rallarens hjelp
— et av de mest besøkte turiststeder i Norge.
Flåmsdalen, today one of the most beloved valleys.
But once considered as «completely impossible» by those
constructing the railway.

Ved Dalsbotn forsvinner elven plutselig ned i undergrunnen.
Fossen minner om en romersk fontene.
Morgenstemning fra ferja Aurland—Gudvangen.
At Dalsbotn the river makes an underground detour.
The waterfall is like a Roman fountain.
Below a glimpse from the morning ferry from Aurland to Gudvangen.

Midt i Jotunheimen. For ikke så mange år siden — en nesten lukket og ukjent verden. ▷
I dag kan fotografen sitte ved Leirvassbu, og i godt vær ta bilder som dette.
Not so many years ago this was unknown inaccessible territory.
Today we can relax at Leirvassbu right in the middle of Jotunheimen,
and wherever we look, more beauty is singing.

Galdhøpiggen sett fra Juvasshytta.
Bildet ble tatt tidlig en morgen da naturen
syntes å være malt i rødt.
Galdhøpiggen getting a rosy
good-morning-kiss from the sun.

Her kan det gå rundt for en — hva er opp og hva er ned?
På vei mot Jotunheimen, et sted i Gudbrandsdalen der stillheten var fullkommen.
Og ikke langt unna det svake suset fra et vannfall som la slør over skogen.
What is up? What is down? The only thing quite clear is the water.
And there is trout to be caught in the Gudbrandsdalen. From not far away
comes the soft murmur of a waterfall: The dance of the seventh veil?

Sollyset leker med Bøverdalen. Sett ovenfra som her,
kan selv karrige små bruk gi en antydning av plantasje.
Bøverdalen. Try the small road up to Raubergstulen,
even if in the beginning it looks vertical.
(But watch out for the big bus!)
Once up, this and so much more is your reward.

Men også oppe i høyfjellet ved Leirvassbu, var grønnfargen uvanlig,
kanskje på grunn av kontrast med snø og fjell.
Llewellyn's sweet title, «How green was my valley»,
could apply to Leirvassbu.

43

Slik lages en elv. Først et lite bekkesilder
fra et myrsøkk eller en vannpytt høyere oppe i fjellet
— eller ørsmå tilsig av vanndråper fra solvarmet snø.
The birth of a river! This little trickle, from sunwarmed snow,
will soon turn into mighty, roaring falls and rapids.

Kyrkja, så vakker om morgenen, ved middag,
om kvelden, om natten, i storm, i regn, i snø.
Kyrkja. How can a mountain be so incredibly beautiful?
In the morning, at noon, in the evening, come storm, come rain, come snow.

Snøbreen ligger der ganske nær, som den har gjort
siden de første mennesker vandret gjennom landskapet.
Her virker det avvisende kaldt og ugjestmildt.
The glaciers are there, as they have been since the very first man.

Dalen ved Leirvassbu — åpen og innbydende.
The valley at Leirvassbu again, so open and hospitable.

Og like ved Leirvassbu et øye av et vannspeil
og en stor snøfonn som ikke lar seg fordrive
av en kort galning av en sommer!
*And close to Leirvassbu a shimmering small lake
and a finger of a glacier which won't be moved away
by some short-lived madman called «Summer».*

46

Hva mer kan en ønske seg enn å slå opp øynene en morgen,
se vasen med markblomster som en pike har satt i din vinduskarm,
og så la øynene favne inn den hele verden,
perfekt innrammet av vinduskarmene?
What more can one ask for, than to rise in the morning to this view?
Including the little vase of mountain flowers,
greeting me as I entered my room. Leirvassbu.

Lyset leker seg i vann og stein ved Kyrkja og Leirvassbu.
The light having fun at Leirvassbu.

«Skynd deg! Skynd deg! Fly som en hind!
Se hvor det griner bak Fanaråktind,»
skrev Henrik Wergeland i «Spaniolen»
— tydelig inspirert av sin tur over Sognefjellet.
«Hurry, hurry, run like a deer!
The gust behind Fanatind is already here.»
wrote Henrik Wergeland in «Spaniolen»,
— obviously inspired by his tour over the mountain Sognefjellet.

Som Moldau gav Smetana inspirasjon til et symfonisk dikt,
skulle vel dette vassfaret gi inspirasjon til et operaverk.
Smetana's «Moldau», but here with a very Norwegian bouquet.

Også Henrik Ibsen drog over Sognefjell.
Kanskje var det den turen han mintes,
da han skrev om en tinderad — lik en fylking
av hærkledte troll bak flikete jøkler.
Henrik Ibsen also walked over the Sognefjellet,
a tour forever impressed on his memory,
later referred to in his works.

51

Veien opp Jostedalen til Nigardsbreen er som å følge
en malers vei fram til den absolutte renhet og enkelhet.
Finere luft enn her finnes vel ikke. Sikten er så ufattelig
at man synes å kunne se inn i fremtiden.
The road up to Nigardsbreen is like following the ways
of a painter, up to absolute purity and simplicity.
The air so pure and the visibility so unbelievably clear,
it seems possible to look into the future.

Morgentåken begynte å lette ved Dombås. Kunne man i et bilde fange noe ▷
av den selsomme blandingen av mykhet og klarhet før den rakk å forsvinne?
This morning mist started to disappear at Dombås. Could I capture
the rare mixture of softness and clarity, before it all went away?

Underlige formasjoner av is flyter majestetisk nedover
fra brefronten. En grasiøs svane — eller er det tre forskjellige?
En and med hodet i vannet, en anrettet kalkun?
Strange formations of ice, serenely floating downwards.
A gracious swan? A duck hunting food at the bottom?
Or a turkey for Thanksgiving Day?

Fruktbare Stardalen — som et alpedalføre med en grønnfarge
som man vel ellers bare ser på irske turistplakater. Og bak
de hengebratte fjellene glimter det av og til fra Jostedalsbreen.
— Vest for breen en utløper ved Briksdal ovenfor Oldevatnet.
Braket fra den kalvende isen sier: Hit, men ikke lenger!
Stardalen may confuse you: Are you in Ireland's Kerry,
or in France's Loire-valley? But a glimpse of the mighty
Jostedalsbreen quickly puts you right again.
Briksdalen is another valley, to the west of Jostedalsbreen
where the thunder from the breaking glacier tells you where to stop.

Og plutselig stanser man opp på sin vandring til Briksdalsbreen,
på grunn av en bagatell, et mirakel: Tre tistler som en hellig treenighet,
eller som en bukett skjenket av overgartneren.
Dead stop, on my way to the glacier at Briksdal:
The miraculous bagatelle of three thistles as a Holy Trinity.

Slik møter Briksdalen den som orker å trave så langt
— som et minne fra en glemt urtid, da snø av dette slaget
dekket hele Norge. — Nedenfor brefronten smelter
iskossene eller blir knust til smått av strykene.
It is not easy to reach this spot at Briksdal.
But once there, one's thoughts go back to the beginning of time,
when ice like this covered the whole of Norway.
— But the ice-age is gone, here the glacier turns into a river.

Innviksfjorden ved Stryn, en viktig ferdselsåre
og et eventyr av skjønnhet.
Beautiful Innviksfjorden, close to Stryn.
It takes hours to drive around the dramatic fjord,
and a big heart to house all the impressions.

En septemberdag i Videdalen da fargene spraket med en voldsomhet
som var de blåst ut av tusen trompeter.
*A September-day in Videdalen, where the colours were singing
in fortissimo, as if blown by a thousand trumpets.*

61

Og igjen Videdalen — en julidag da et tåketeppe
hyllet alt inn i en intim taushet.
Videdalen again. A day in July
when thick fog covered up all activities.

Og endelig en fuktig augustdag,
da allnaturen likesom holdt pusten i spenning,
mens den ventet på tordenværet som lå i luften.
A humid August-day, when everything held its breath,
waiting for the thunderstorm building up.

62

Krystallklart vann i stor fart kan gi et vel så sterkt inntrykk
av kraft og liv som skummende fossestryk. Ottaelva ved Pollfoss
byr på alle varianter av vann i hurtig bevegelse.
Pollfoss, on the road to Grotli. Why is it that
fast-running clear water gives a much stronger impression
of power and life, than the foam of even the biggest waterfall?

Geirangerfjorden med Ørneveien. Bondegårder klynger seg fast
langs de ville stupene. Om kveldene kan man se parafinlamper
lyse opp usynlige hus som det ikke finnes noen vei til,
bare nesten loddrette klatrestier. De fleste av disse gårdene
ligger øde nå, men fremdeles er noen bebodd.
The Geirangerfjorden with Ørneveien, «the eagle-road».
A Geiranger-farm from the old days.

Straks man har lagt Grotli bak seg
og satt kursen for Geiranger.
Bare noen minutter etter at jeg var ferdig her,
kom uværet og sopte bort all stillhet.
Soon after Grotli, on the road to Geiranger.
Right when I had taken my picture, a strong wind
immediately swept the tranquility away.

Bildene antyder en «rute» fra Åndalsnes via Trollstigveien til Ålesund.
Her står de i rekke og rad Dronningen, Kongen, Bispen og alle de andre.
Det er så mange av dem disse himmelstrebende tinder, nåler, horn
— hva de nå har fått til navn. Og de skaper en slående kontrast
med sine snøkroner mot den yppige vegetasjon i lune dalsider.
Det forekommer en at husene i Ålesund rettelig hører hjemme
på et maleri av en av de hollandske mestrene.
A quartet, from Åndalsnes, via the road «Trollstigen», to Ålesund.
And here they are, all lined up: The Queen, the King, the Bishop and all the others.
Their snowy crowns in striking contrast to the lush vegetation in the valleys.
The buildings of Ålesund seem rather to be part of a painting by a Dutch master.

Røros — og er det egentlig nødvendig å si noe mer?
Jo, kanskje at gaten øverst til høyre heter Slaggveien,
og at vi i bildet under tar et indiskret blikk inn i Slaggveien 4.
Her kan man føle at man vil møte bergløytnant Dopp, eller Gölin eller Brodde
(fra Johan Falkbergets «Christianus Sextus») like bak neste hushjørne.

Røros, town of the old copper mines. The street is of course named Slaggveien,
the Slag-road, and hopefully the good people living in no. 4, do not mind our peeping
through their windows. Everywhere in Røros one gets the feeling that
around the next corner the mountain-lieutenant Dopp
and all the others, from Johan Falkberget's «Christianus Sextus» are waiting.

Grønt, grønt og fruktbart på Inderøy i Nord-Trøndelag. ▷
Green, lush green, on Inderøy, «the inner island», in Nord-Trøndelag.

Et fjell av sand — en morene — ved Røros. Sand, stein, grus
og slagghauger, kan trenge en kontrast — en issoleie, som for øvrig
kan klare seg fint under barskere forhold enn på Rørosvidda.
*A mountain of sand in Røros — a moraine. And a contrast,
a Ranunculus glacialis, managing well even
under harder conditions than those found on the Rørosvidda.*

Fra bygdeveien ved Norem mot Beitstadfjorden gikk
en smal sidevei til venstre. Her på toppen endte veien
og jeg ble sittende i timer og vente på det helt riktige lyset.
From the road to Norem, at Beitstadfjorden,
there was a small road going up to the left.
It ended right at the top, and for hours I sat there
gratefully, waiting for the right light.

Geometriske form- og fargeblandinger ved Borgenfjorden.
Geometrical shapes and colours at Borgenfjorden.

Det var noe ved denne spesielle kvelden ved Store Majavatn
som tente varslingslampen i meg: Ikke til sengs ennå!
Med utstyret klart spekulerte jeg på hva som, kanskje, skulle komme.
Og det kom: Til langt over midnatt, da jeg knipset
siste bildet, var jeg gjest på en lysfest!
This very evening, at Store Majavatn, something caused
my warnings-lights to flash: «Do not go to bed yet!» With everything
at the ready, I wondered what could possibly come.
It came: Until early morning, when I made the
last picture, I was guest at a fantastic light-party.

Ettermiddag ved Store Majavatn.
Og så et hopp gjennom Vefsn og over Korgfjellet
til Leirskardalen innunder Okstindane.
Late afternoon at Store Majavatn. — And a good jump,
through Vefsn and over Korgfjellet,
to the valley of Leirskardalen,
right below the Okstindane.

Leirskardalen byr ikke på brak og dunder
som i en Wagner-opera, men på herlig og rent kvartett-spill
som et kammermusikalsk filigransarbeid.
The Leirskardalen does not give you the crashing thunder
of a Wagner-opera, but lovely, pure quartet playing,
like a piece of chamber-musical filigree-work.

84

Strømvirvlene fra Saltstraumen sprer seg
utover den blanke Saltfjorden.
*Saltstraumen, where the tide dramatically empties
and fills a huge fjord through this narrow strait.*

Der sto fjellet og vinket med toppen. Men vinkingen var nok ikke
bestemt for meg, men for et enda vakrere fjell langt bak meg.
Ved Tjorvihytta sør for Sulitjelma.
*Do mountains chat? Of course they do, by waving their peaks at each other.
Like this one, down at Tjorvihytta, south of Sulitjelma.*

To ganger hadde jeg strevd meg opp den bratte veien høyt
ovenfor Straumvatnet, men været hadde lurt meg begge ganger.
På den tredje turen fikk jeg en belønning.
Twice I tried to get up the steep road,
high above the Straumvatnet, but bad weather stopped me.
The prize was awarded upon my third attempt.

Kråkmotinden vokter over fjell og vann i et vilt — og smilende landskap.
The Kråkmotinden, keeping watch over a really wild country.

«Vann som renner, vann som risler,
Vann om våren, vann om høsten,
Vann i Norge, vann av renhet.»
«Racing waters, singing waters,
young in the spring, young in the autumn,
Norway's waters, purity's praise.»
(Nordahl Grieg)

På vei inn i Knut Hamsuns land, så jeg denne Hamarøy-båten hvile,
som om den skulle vært plassert nøyaktig der av en av de store malerne.
On my way into Knut Hamsun's land, I saw this Hamarøy-boat resting,
as if put there by one of the great painters.

Ouverturen til Lofoten er komponert over det samme fine tema
enten en kommer dit pr. båt, i bil eller med vanlig ferje.
Her en ettermiddagspastorale med fjære sjø ved Herjangsfjorden.
*The overture to the Lofoten is composed around the
same, fine theme, whether you arrive by car or by ferry.
Here an afternoon-pastoral at low tide, from the Herjangsfjorden.*

Den røde Flakstad kirke, ydmykt stående ved foten av
Guds eget skaperverk på den andre siden av fjorden.
*The red church of Flakstad, humbly bowing
to God's own creation across the fjord.*

Lengst inne i Flakstadpollen finnes et ørlite fall,
ikke stort mer enn en bekk, som generøst leverer
sitt brevann direkte til havet.
*At the bottom of the Flakstad-pool, this tiny brook
proudly delivers its melted snow directly to the sea.*

Og så fortsetter turen ned til Nusfjord,
der lyset finner et drømmested for sine evige blindebukkstreker
— senere tar også månen del i leken.
*While we continue towards Nusfjord, where the light has found
an ideal place for its eternal game of blindman's buff.
In which the moon, too, takes part.*

En kontrastrik bukett av skjønnhet tilsatt Lofotens spesielle, myke lys.
De store linjer i landskapet er ville og forrevne,
men i det små finnes legio av viker og odder å utforske. Flakstadøy.
Make a bouquet of contrasts from nature's own, wild beauty.
Add to it the soft, sweet light of Lofoten. And within
the now and then threatening landscape, you will find an endless number
of small creeks and points to be explored. The Flakstadøy.

Storvask — underveis til Stamsund — også av en ullen sommertåke
som flagret lett i synsranden som om den hang til tørk.
Time for the big spring-cleaning, on the way to Stamsund.
Including the woollen summer-fog with everything hung up to dry.

Fra Vestvågøy mot Ballstad-fjellene. ▷
From Vestvågøy towards the Ballstad mountain.

Ved Sildpollen-kapellet ble det bråstopp.
Hvis det er meningen at jeg skal få med bare et eneste
bilde fra Lofoten, så la det bli dette!
Dead stop at the Sildpollen-chapel: If I am to bring home
just one single picture from the whole of Lofoten,
then please let it be this one.

En ventende båt gjør stillheten fullkommen.
A waiting boat in complete calm.

Og så driver uværet unna på Vestvågøy.
Be gone, bad weather, away you go! The Vestvågøy.

Midnatt på Hadseløya i Vesterålen.
Midnight at the Hadseløya, in the Vesterålen.

Stillheten var fullkommen, og plutselig løsnet
de store tåkebankene fra horisonten.
Over alt omkring meg skinte det, mens værgudene moret seg med,
noen ganger skarpt, å spille med lyset.
Peace was complete, and suddenly huge banks of clouds and fog
broke away from the horizon. And all around me it shimmered and flashed softly.
— The weather-gods were having fun, playing with the light.

Det er selskap i måsene — det er mange av dem i Vesterålen.
Iblant utplassert på takene som av en nøyeregnende ballettmester,
iblant sammentrengt på spesielle steiner ute i sjøen,
selv om det vrimler av fugletomme, men tilsynelatende identiske steiner rundt om.
Seagulls are company, and much company is found in the Vesterålen.
Sometimes they are lined up on a roof, as if trained by a demanding ballet-master.
And sometimes they are crowded on special rocks in the sea,
with a lot of identical but completely deserted rocks all around them.

Måsene protesterte høylydt mot at jeg frekt løftet på nettet
og kløv inn — de var jo enda ikke ferdig med frokosten!
Med hver sin godbit i nebbet forsvant de ut gjennom
et stort hull i nettet, og satte seg så utenfor og hånet meg.
The sea-gulls protested noisily at the intruder,
lifting the net and entering. They came out through a hole in the netting,
each one with a dainty morsel, and started chiding me.

Selvsagt har en fiskebåt en sjel, og selvsagt kan den søve.
I Grimstad, i Vinje og i alle de andre havnene,
ligger de der og drømmer om hvor fint livet kunne være.
Of course a fishing-boat has a soul,
and of course it needs sleep! In Grimstad, in Vinje,
in all the fishing-ports, there they are,
fast asleep and dreaming of a peaceful life.

113

Det er fjellet Reka som dominerer landskapet
på denne delen av Langøya.
On my way to the little ferry at Sandset (Vesterålen), the mountain Reka,
«the Shrimp», beckoned and called: «Hey, don't I rate a picture?»
Ah, but of course! My humble apologies.

Fra Utskår, tvers over Malnesfjorden, får man øye på dette lille huset
i oppkjeftig ensomhet og blir nysgjerrig etter å få vite
hvem som har gjort det lille stedet til en del av sin livsfilosofi.
From Utskår, over the Malnesfjord, this little cottage is seen
in its defiant solitude. One gets curious as to who
made this place a part of his philosophy.

115

Søndagsfred i Vesterålen.
Nær Kråkberget og ved Nykvåg, ytterst mot storhavet.
Still life at Vesterålen, Sunday.
Near the Crow-hill and Nykvåg, farthest out towards the deep sea.

Måsene er på besøk i sitt spiskammer.
Trangt om plassen kan det bli.
Grand gala-dinner. White tie and tails, yes.
Formal seating etc., no.

Ved Alsvåg tar en farvel med både Vesterålen og Lofoten,
mens ettermiddagssolen får Langøya til å glitre.
Good bye, dear Vesterålen. So long, my darling Lofoten!
As the evening-sun sparkles on the Langøya.

Målselvfossen synes først å være et eneste stort,
hvitt og kontinuerlig brøl, men ved laksetrappen kan man likevel
småprate med giganten.
At first Målselvfossen seems to be just an enormous,
white and interminable thundering, but at the salmon ladder
a good place is found for small talk with the giant.

Pastorale ved Barduelva
og et glimt fra den skjønne Signaldalen ved Otertind.
Pastoral at the Barduelva, and a glimpse
of the beautiful Signaldalen, with the Otertind.

126

På vei nordover langs Lyngenfjorden, — en sonatine av et fossefall.
Enda et bilde av dobbeltpyramiden Otertind i Signaldalen
— og et utsyn over Skjervøy.
Northbound along the Lyngenfjorden. The sonatina of a
brook's fall while the wild Lyng-alps are hidden in haze.
Again the double pyramid of the Otertind in Signaldalen.
— And the first view of Skjervøy.

Det er vår i Skjervøy, og de beryktede uværene fra Lopphavet holder pusten.
Men Kågtinden og Kvænangstindan bærer ennå lite av vårbud i seg
der de vil være med som bakgrunn overalt.
*Springtime in Skjervøy, with the notorious storms from the Lopphavet
holding their breath. The Kågtinden and the Kvænangstindan are real lens-bugs,
trying to get into every picture, but as messengers of spring they are somewhat late.*

131

Ved Alteidet går en liten vei til Jøkelfjorden, en arm av Kvænangen.
Utsyn mot Langnesfjellet og Kvænangsfjellet.
En same i sin båt — ellers så stille.
From Alteidet there is a small road to the Jøkelfjorden, an arm of Kvænangen.
Do not miss it! — Here the Langnesfjellet and the Kvænangstindan.
And a Lapp, going to look for his reindeer across the fjord.

133

Den gamle, lykkelige veien til Gargia fjellstue.
The old, happy road to the charming Gargia fjell-station.

Gargiaelva før den munner ut i Altaelva.
The Gargia river, just before it drops down into the Altaelva.

Igjen ved Gargia fjellstue med veien som ble bygget før gamleveien.
Og Trangdalselva. Sier man farvel til elvene ved Gargia?
Once again at the Gargia fjell-station. And the road that was built long before
the old road. Trangdalselva, the «river of the narrow valley»,
proudly showing off. And with one more sad farewell.

Fuktig morgen i Vardø havn.
Og et gløtt av sol ovenfor Tana bru.
Bildet fra Kobbholmsfjorden ved Grense Jakobselv
er veis ende.
Wet morning in the port of Vardø.
A stingy sun, and a cutting wind, near the Tana bridge.
The end of the road: The Kobbholmsfjorden at Grense Jakobselv.

Fotografen selv — og datoen er 5. juni.
The photographer himself, — the date is June 5.